T0053321

GATHERING THE GOODNESS
OF GOD'S WORD

STUDY GUIDE plus STREAMING VIDEO

SIX SESSIONS

KRISTY CAMBRON

HarperChristian Resources

Verse Mapping Bible Study: Luke, Gathering the Goodness of God's Word
© 2018 by Kristy Cambron

Requests for information should be addressed to:
HarperChristian Resources, 3900 Sparks Dr. SE, Grand Rapids, Michigan 49546

ISBN 978-0-310-08989-6 (softcover)
ISBN 978-0-310-08990-2 (ebook)

Published in association with Books & Such Literary Management, 52 Mission Circle, Suite 122, PMB 170, Santa Rosa, California 95409-5370, www.booksandsuch.com.

Photo on page 128 © Shutterstock.

First Printing March 2018 / Printed in the United States of America

Contents

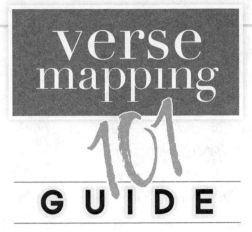

Steps to Study the Bible Like Never Before

WHY VERSE MAPPING?

Let's be honest—does anyone else have difficulty understanding Scripture? *(Waving hand over here . . .)*

Do you want to do more than just read—you actually want to research and apply what's in the Bible to your life today? *(Me too! Waving again.)*

Are you looking for a fellowship community where you can read, learn, explore, and map the Word of God together? *(Still here!)*

If this is you too, and you love unpacking the context of the Scriptures you're reading, but you want to do it in a super-simple way—looking at the Hebrew/Greek translations, finding connections in the Word, and learning as much as you can from your time with the Holy Spirit—then get ready. . . . You've just joined the community study that will inspire, encourage, and unlock your understanding of the Word of God!

WHAT IS VERSE MAPPING?

Verse mapping isn't new. It's been a topic of conversation for years. You'll find endless examples with a simple online search. And you guessed it—Bible journaling images and methods are popping up all over social media. But what is verse mapping? Who's doing it? And can it really help you understand the Word more clearly?

First things first . . .

definition: *Verse mapping is a method of studying the historical context, transliteration, translation, connotation, and theological framework of a verse (or section of verses) in the Bible.*

Plain and simple? Verse mapping is getting real about studying the Bible. All of it. It's not just reading. It's researching everything you can in a verse to learn more about who God is and how He wants to speak to you through His Word. In short? It's serious study.

4 actions
What actions develop the story in this verse? What is happening in this verse? To whom?

1 verse
What verse am I mapping? What key themes or specific words are speaking to me today?

2 design ———— **develop 3**

What different translations make up the design for this verse? Underline key phrases or words repeated.

What is the Hebrew or Greek meaning for the underlined phrases or words?

5 outcome ————
What is God saying to me today? How do I apply this to my life?

HOW-TO FOR BEGINNERS

What qualifies me to do this kind of study?

If you're not a seminary-trained theologian by education, don't worry—verse mapping is for anyone with a heart to know the Word of God more.

What matters is not how much knowledge you have before you begin, but where the experience takes you. Verse mapping will inspire you to dig into the Word of God in individual study and in a group setting like never before. The Holy Spirit is your teacher and companion in this study; it's not the *what* you bring to the table that qualifies you—it's *Who*. And He's going to make sure you learn no matter where you begin.

What are the rules?

- **Rule #1:** If you can't back up your conclusions or thoughts with Scripture, then you can't write it down. Everything is fair game in studying *as long as God said it first*. (In other words, don't make anything up and don't assume you know what something means— back it up with Scripture or go back and find the *real* answer.)

- **Rule #2:** Make it personal. This is your journal and your study time with God. More than anything, let God meet you in this unique and intimate space and speak to you.

- **Rule #3:** Keep to your preferences for verse mapping—if you like to highlight . . . if you like to use a specific marker/pen color . . . or if you like to circle or underline key words and phrases. Do what feels intuitive for you.

There's no structurally right or wrong way to verse map. This particular study is structured working from right to left (a documentation page on the right, notes page on the left), and top to bottom. Once you've gathered the tools and mastered the confidence to apply what you've learned, it's up to you how your journal will look. Focus on the process and the way of this study method. Learn how to read and ask at the same time, and then go find the answers.

GATHERING AND GETTING STARTED

This section is quick. It's all about gathering a handful of tools and readying your heart for Him.

What you will need

Whether you're at a desk in your home office, at the local coffee shop, or on the go, verse mapping is a study method that will move with you. In fact, you probably already carry everything you need just about anywhere you go:

- **Journal:** Verse Mapping study guide with blank maps, or a notebook with blank pages.

- **Markers/pens:** Specific colors of markers or pens aren't required. This is personal.

- **Bible:** Or a Bible app on a smart device (to look up various translations).

- **Concordance:** Select a concordance with Hebrew/Greek dictionaries. I recommend *The NIV Exhaustive Bible Concordance, Third Edition* from Zondervan, but you can also find the information online. If you don't have one—or if you're not able to carry one with you—you can also find this information on your smart device.

- **Time (varies):** While it's a requirement, the time you block on your calendar is *up to you*. Study time is on the honor system between you and God. If you have five minutes today and an hour tomorrow, dedicate what time you can, when you can. It's all about communion with Him.

Study Prompt

Time is a big factor. You may have others who depend on you either inside your home, outside it, or both—and that can cut into the time you're able to study. If finding study *time* is a struggle that becomes a burden, then add that into the next step and pray about it. Eventually, you won't have to carve out time in the Word; it will be what your heart craves first, and most. The time to study will follow the passion to learn.

Prayer

This is a Holy Spirit-led study. So pray. Talk to Him. Ask Him to reveal more of who He is through your verse mapping journey.

The Holy Spirit must be the active guide in any time of study. Do whatever works to invite Him into your study space (listen to worship music, close the door, turn off all sound). Pray before every single time you open your Bible and intentionally seek deeper and clearer understanding of what you will read.

MAPPING 101

A comprehensive guide to change-your-life study time with God.

The process is simple. Each of the following words corresponds to a section on your verse map. Here's what you do (after you pray!):

- **Verse:** Select and write your verse(s) to map. Include the translation

- **Design:** Write your verse(s) in two to four different translations. Identify key words or phrases that stand out among the varying translations.

- **Develop:** Look up key words or phrases in Hebrew/Greek. Write down definitions, synonyms, and root words. Discover any underlying meaning(s) in verse(s) and note it. (See the Reference and Resource Guide at the back of this study guide if you need help with where to look words up.)

- **Actions:** Research and document the people, places, and the context referenced. Ask: Who? What? Where? When? Why? How? Note connections to other concepts in Scripture you are familiar with and/or find in your research.

- **Outcome:** Write a one- to two-sentence summary of what you've learned. Anchor the verse you mapped to your life. This is the treasured truth the map brought you to.

That's it—five simple steps to change-your-life study time with God! All set? Let's map.

⇒ THE MAP ⇐

4 actions
What actions develop the story in this verse? What is happening in this verse? To whom?

1 verse
What verse am I mapping? What key themes or specific words are speaking to me today?

WRITE YOUR VERSE(S) –

WHAT IS THE HOLY SPIRIT TEACHING ME?

2 design ——— **develop 3**

What different translations make up the design for this verse? Underline key phrases or words repeated.

What is the Hebrew or Greek meaning for the underlined phrases or words?

5 outcome ——————
What is God saying to me today? How do I apply this to my life?

1 verse

Select your verse(s)

Everything in your map will hinge on what verse(s) you select. Whether you're reading through an entire book of the Bible or moving around through a verse(s) of a specific theme, this is where you choose what your path will be for your study time. A few questions to ask yourself as you read:

- *What grabs me when I read it?*

- *What themes do I see?*

- *What question(s) do I have about what I just read?*

Write your verse(s)

If something stands out, then you can be sure that's your verse(s) for the day. Select it and write it down.

This study is formatted for use with the New International Version of the Bible. However, you can choose which translation(s) you prefer most. Once you've selected the verse(s) you'll map, write it in your preferred translation. (Remember, you'll document it in at least two to four other translations next.)

Study Prompt

What verse are you mapping? What key themes or specific words are speaking to you today?

- *What's on your heart today?* If you're facing a difficult circumstance, or find yourself in an unexpected path in your own story with God, select a verse(s) that speaks to the theme of your heart for today.

- *What's that word?* If you're reading Scripture and something jumps off the page—a word you don't recognize, a city you've never heard of, or a phrase you don't quite understand—this is a good indication it might be your verse(s) to map for the day.

Everything in your map will hinge on what verse(s) you select.

Study Prompt

What gets lost in translation? How do the different translations present the same ideas or biblical principles?

4 actions — What actions develop the story in this verse? What is happening in this verse? To whom?

1 verse — What verse am I mapping? What key themes or specific words are speaking to me today?

2 design ———————— **develop 3**

What different translations make up the design for this verse? Underline key phrases or words repeated.

What is the Hebrew or Greek meaning for the underlined phrases or words?

5 outcome — What is God saying to me today? How do I apply this to my life?

WRITE YOUR VERSE IN MULTIPLE TRANSLATIONS

—

WHAT DOES THIS VERSE SAY?

2 design

The *design* identifies what the verse is calling attention to by comparing translations. The *design* calls out similar word choice, repetition of words, phrases, and/or aspects of grammar common across multiple translations. It brings to light what the verse is saying that cannot be lost to translation, and what may stand out as translation specific. Anything here could trigger a question or path for further investigation.

Write your verse(s)—or selected phrase(s)—in two to four additional translations. Underline, circle, or highlight key phrases or words that may be repeated across multiple translations.

④ actions — What actions develop the story in this verse? What is happening in this verse? To whom?

① verse — What verse am I mapping? What key themes or specific words are speaking to me today?

② design ———————— **develop ③**

What different translations make up the design for this verse? Underline key phrases or words repeated.

What is the Hebrew or Greek meaning for the underlined phrases or words?

RESEARCH & WRITE KEY WORD MEANINGS (HEBREW or GREEK)

—

WHAT DOES THIS VERSE MEAN?

⑤ outcome ————————
What is God saying to me today? How do I apply this to my life?

③ develop

Develop why and how the verse, key word(s), or idea is important through Hebrew (Old Testament) or Greek (New Testament) word research, definitions, and comparisons. Dig deeper. Use a concordance and online word search databases. Look up the meanings of your key words or phrases and write them down.

Note word choice, part(s) of speech, and find some seriously cool context around your verse.

If a word is used across all translations, find out why. If the verse moves from past tense (something that's already happened) to present tense (something that's ongoing), find out why. If a Greek word was used in one translation and not another . . . find out why.

- **Old Testament verses**—research the Hebrew.

    Example: S. 6213. *asah* (aw-saw) a primitive root; to do or make, in the broadest sense and widest application (as follows):—accomplish, advance, appoint

- **New Testament verses**—research the Greek.

    Example: S. 4100. *pisteuó* (pist-yoo'-o) from 4102; to have faith (in, upon, or with respect to, a person or thing), i.e. credit; by implication, to entrust (especially one's spiritual well-being to Christ):—believe(-r), commit (to trust), put in trust with

    Note: S. is an abbreviation for *The NIV Exhaustive Concordance.*

Study Prompt

Look at the verse in context. Think like a storyteller—how would you explain what's happening in your verse? Find the five senses in the story—sight, smell, sound, taste, and touch—as if you stepped into the characters' shoes. Look at what occurred before and after your verse. What's happening that caused the action in your verse?

 Verse mapping is getting real about studying the Bible.

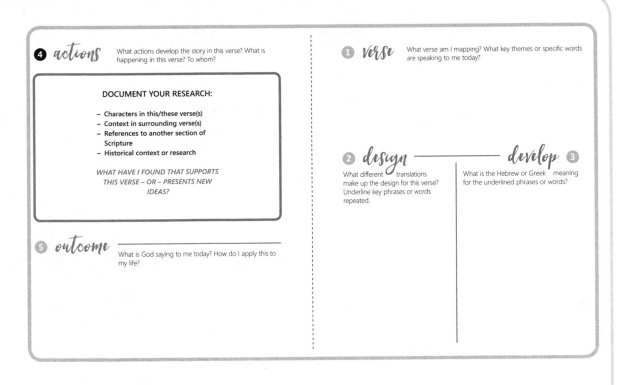

④ actions — What actions develop the story in this verse? What is happening in this verse? To whom?

DOCUMENT YOUR RESEARCH:

– Characters in this/these verse(s)
– Context in surrounding verse(s)
– References to another section of Scripture
– Historical context or research

WHAT HAVE I FOUND THAT SUPPORTS THIS VERSE – OR – PRESENTS NEW IDEAS?

① verse — What verse am I mapping? What key themes or specific words are speaking to me today?

② design ———— develop ③

What different translations make up the design for this verse? Underline key phrases or words repeated.

What is the Hebrew or Greek meaning for the underlined phrases or words?

⑤ outcome — What is God saying to me today? How do I apply this to my life?

④ actions

Actions record:

- What's happening in the verse

- Who the characters are in what you're reading

- How their story relates to other stories/verses/persons in other areas of Scripture

- What are the topics, themes, dates of significant events, and/or theological elements of the verse(s) you're researching

Anything is fair game here, as long as you can back it up with Scripture. Look back a few chapters or verses and read what precedes your verse(s). Identify who, what, where, when. Research the context and customs of what life would have been like for the characters in your verse(s). Look up maps. Open history books. Read about what happened, why it happened, and how it is relevant to your life today.

This is where you'll find how the story connects to *your* story with God. Research it and write it down.

4 actions
What actions develop the story in this verse? What is happening in this verse? To whom?

1 verse
What verse am I mapping? What key themes or specific words are speaking to me today?

2 design
What different translations make up the design for this verse? Underline key phrases or words repeated.

3 develop
What is the Hebrew or Greek meaning for the underlined phrases or words?

5 outcome
What is God saying to me today? How do I apply this to my life?

WRITE YOUR MAP SUMMARY FOR
FUTURE USE —

WHAT HAVE I LEARNED?
(LIFE APPLICATION)

5 outcome

The *outcome* is a quick-hit summary of what you've learned. One or two sentences should do it. Summarize, jot it down, and come back later to find where the Holy Spirit has confirmed His promises to you. This is your claim on this verse, at this time of your life. The *outcome* should reflect whatever truth has been revealed in your map.

Study Prompt

As you continue verse mapping, you'll find this is the section that you refer back to most often. Summarize what you've learned—how would you take this truth and apply it in your home, office, school, church, or community? Make it short and powerful.

SPECIAL NOTE

Don't be afraid to start small.

If your first maps are one or two pages with lots of white space, that's okay. Other maps (depending on what you need to hear from God that day) could turn into four pages of study that digs deep into your heart.

Look up a word here. Choose a verse there. Just do it honestly, and the Holy Spirit will grow your passion around His Word. You don't have to have it all figured out with the first or even the twentieth map. You just have to come hungry to the table every day. God will handle the preparation for the feast ahead of time.

So, now it's your turn! Want to give it a try? Join the *community* of other Jesus-chasing mappers out there. Be sure to use the hashtag #VerseMapClub to connect and share your verse-map experience on social media. I'll be adding more posts soon, and you can bet I'll want to see how it's going for you. Connect with me on social media—I'm heart-happy to take this journey with you!

Kristy

She Believed

"Blessed is she who has believed that the Lord would fulfill His promises to her!"

LUKE 1:45

OPENING REFLECTION

These words in Luke 1:45 were spoken about a young girl named Mary, who received a promise of God's goodness—that she'd been chosen to bear a child who was and is the Savior of the world. But it was still her choice to believe, and her faith that would have to anchor her through all that was to come after. It's not all that different from what we face today—the choice to believe over the weight of our circumstances, and the faith to carry us as we charge headlong into them.

What if there were no barriers to faith? What if we could study God's promises, understand, and apply the Word to our daily lives, believing God will fulfill all He's promised?

What if the things that seem *impossible* on our own suddenly became *possible* with God?

GATHERING AND GETTING STARTED

Welcome to the first session of *Luke: Gathering the Goodness of God's Word*.

Whether you're meeting in a coffee shop corner, a church fellowship hall, in your home, or even on your neighbor's front porch, this is meant to be a *gathering study*. It should be relatable and relaxed—a place to talk faith, life, and story roads—and invite the Holy Spirit into your day by opening the Word of God in the spaces you naturally gather.

If this is the first time you've gathered together, take a few moments to get to know your group. Introduce yourself with something as simple as your name and why you've come to study God's Word. And if you want to jump in to get things started, discuss one of the following questions:

● *What do you know about verse mapping? What do you hope to learn on this verse mapping journey?*

or

● *What's your biggest barrier to overcome in studying God's Word? Is it a lack of time? Knowledge? Or something else?*

GATHERING: VIDEO STORY

Play the video segment for session one. As you watch, follow the verse mapping guide points starting below and refer to the completed map on pages 22–23. Take brief notes or record questions that might lead you to further research in your independent study time this week.

Notes

1 *verse*

What makes the Gospel of Luke unique:

Only Gospel addressed to a specific person—Theophilus, who was likely a Gentile believer like Luke (see Colossians 4)

Most lengthy of the Gospels—presenting a thorough picture of Jesus' ministry (Luke 9–19 chronicle healings and intense teaching, like the Good Samaritan and Mustard Seed parables)

Only Gospel with a sequel—the book of Acts. In both, we find the only detailed accounts of Jesus' ascension.

2 *design*

Faith (she who has believed) partners with God's *promises* (for there will be a fulfillment)

3 *develop*

In the Greek, "believed" is *pisteuó,* meaning "to trust," or entrusted, "to affirm," or have confidence in

In the Greek, "blessed" indicates "the favor of God"

Under the favor of God is she who entrusted, having confidence that the action of *fulfillment* will follow that trust

4 *actions*

Mary's belief—her entrusting an unknown future to God—appears in Luke 1:26–38

Mary's response to the angel's news that she would carry a son—the Savior of the world: "I am the Lord's servant" (Luke 1:38)

Mary's lineage of faith—the *blessed is she who believed* women—came in Matthew 1

5 *outcome*

When everything we thought we had—that list of "somethings"—is being chipped away, we can remember that *faith* triggers the blessing

4  *What if there were no barriers to our faith?*

Mary's belief— *Her entrusting an unknown future to God*
(Luke 1:26–38)

- *She received the visit from the angel who said she would give birth to the Messiah—the one who said, "For with God, nothing will be impossible"* **(verse 37 NKJV)**

Mary's response: *Response to the angel's news that she would carry a son—the Savior of the world? She said, "I am the Lord's servant."* **(verse 38 NIV)**

- *Represented her choice to overcome the barrier of the unknown, because her FAITH was rooted in God*

Lineage of Christ: *Found in* **Matthew 1**—*other "BLESSED is she who BELIEVED women" . . . Tamar, Rahab, Ruth, the wife of Uriah . . . and Mary.*

5 *outcome* ────────────

Who Jesus became and what He fulfilled were in part triggered by the blessing—the favor of God on the world—and in "she who BELIEVED."

① *verse* — LUKE 1:45 (NIV)

"Blessed is she who has believed that the Lord would fulfill His promises to her!"

② *design* — *develop* ③

② design

- **NKJV:** *"Blessed is she who <u>believed</u>, for there will be a <u>fulfillment</u> of those things which were told her from the Lord."*

③ develop

- **BELIEVED**—*pisteuó (S. 4100):*

  "to trust," or entrusted; "to affirm," or have confidence in

- **BLESSED**—*Happy. Fortunate. Those feel-good feelings when something works out to our benefit.*

  "Under the favor of God is she who entrusted, having confidence that the action of FULFILLMENT will follow that trust."

  Not just happy. More than fortunate. Under the favor of God, because the belief (the affirmation, or confidence in) triggers the action to fulfill it.

▶| From the Video |◀

"Your time at this company is done."

It was so clear. So strong. And so completely terrifying . . . that for an employee who hadn't a doubt in nearly a decade and a half, I thought I was about to receive my walking papers right there. And in a way, I did.

The mirror-image of who I was on my own, and the vision of who God could make me if I truly surrendered everything—they were at fierce battle. It was Jesus calling out to this worker. Busy in her boat. Fishing for the accolades of the world. Instead, He summoned the "storyteller-at-heart" part of me to experience a completely different story with Him.

. . . After a slow build and years of prayer—that small, nagging, flicker of a flame on my heart to step out and truly follow Jesus? It caught fire. My husband and I felt the call to leave the world we'd built up on our own and step out on a new story road. Kind of like stepping from a boat into the deep . . . or walking a road you never thought you'd travel . . . or trusting God to lead even though you don't have all the answers or even the complete roadmap in front of you.

So I resigned from my picture-perfect, modern high-rise professional job.

I believed that day in the office that God would fulfill His words to me.

GATHERING: GROUP DISCUSSION

Take a few moments with your group to discuss the video you just watched and explore these concepts in Scripture.

1. Think about Luke's profession. How would his education, experience as a physician, and his travels with the apostle Paul aid him to research and record Jesus' earthly ministry? How can your own diverse experiences help you to become researchers in the Word?

   _____

   _____

   _____

2. Select a volunteer to read Luke 1:26–38 aloud to the group. What faith barriers did Mary face in order to trust God with the news the angel had brought? How do some of those same barriers affect your own faith walk?

   _____

   _____

   _____

3. *"Jesus + nothing = everything"* is a key statement to describe Mary's faith walk in this session. What makes this statement true for Mary? Describe a time when you were in a place where Jesus was all you had. What makes it true for you?

   _____

   _____

   _____

   _____

   _____

4. How do the two key words in Luke 1:45—"believed" and "fulfill"—work together to build your faith against seemingly impossible odds?

_____

_____

_____

GATHERING: GROUP ACTIVITY

For this activity, you will need a Bible, pens/markers, and a smart device (such as a phone or tablet).

- Using a Bible or Bible app on a smart device, look up two additional translations of Luke 1:45 and record them on the completed map on pages 22–23.

- To start your verse mapping journey, pray as a group and select one verse you'll map from Luke 1–2 in individual study time this week. Gather in the next session and discuss how your map is similar or different from others' maps.

GATHERING: CLOSING PRAYER

Verse mapping always begins and ends . . . with _prayer_. Gather together with open hearts, expecting the Holy Spirit to remove the barriers to your faith. Ask Him to open the Word of God in your life like never before.

Verse mapping always begins and ends . . . with prayer.

INDIVIDUAL STUDY

⇒ She Believed ⇐

"Blessed is she who has believed that the Lord would fulfill His promises to her!"

LUKE 1:45

The ultimate promise from Luke 1:45 is that the favor—the *blessed* portion of your own story—has already been fulfilled. It was and is fulfilled in the person of Jesus Christ. So here's your invitation until you gather with your group again.

GATHER: INDIVIDUAL STUDY INVITATION

Before you stop to pray . . . before you pick up the pen . . . before you take that first breath and first step on this mapping journey . . . pause.

This will be a marked moment for you—when your heart went from "I wonder if I could?" in understanding God's Word, to "She who believed!" by embarking on your first maps in Luke 1–2.

This is the chain-busting, freedom-seeking, step-out day that you'll look back on as the one in which you chose to explore the announcement of a prophetic birth (1:26–38). To engage your heart in the journey of a young couple on the road to Nazareth (2:4–5). To ask and seek answers of a baby born, who grows in wisdom and favor (2:51–52). To hunger for more of Jesus. Let this be the memory of the very first time you gathered the goodness of His Word in this way.

Pause to savor it . . . then GO.

Gather

INDIVIDUAL STUDY SUPPORT

If this is your first time verse mapping, you may need a couple of prompts to get started. Or refer back to the Verse Mapping 101 Guide at the beginning of your study guide.

1 *verse*
What verse am I mapping? What key themes or specific words are speaking to me today?

2 *design*
What different translations make up the design for this verse? Underline key phrases or words that are repeated across different translations.

3 *develop*
What is the Hebrew or Greek meaning for the underlined phrases or words?

4 *actions*
What actions develop the story in this verse? What is happening in this verse? To whom?

5 *outcome*
Review your map from beginning to end. Notice what God is saying to you through the verse map. How does this truth apply to your life?

Read

LUKE 1 – 2

Take time this week—whether five minutes today or an hour tomorrow—to dive into the Word.

Pray and invite the Holy Spirit into your time in the Word. When you are ready, turn to one of the blank verse maps in this section.

Read Luke 1–2. Select and map verses that speak to your heart. If your group selected a verse to map and discuss together, map that verse this week as well. Prepare to discuss what you've learned when your group gathers again.

Study Prompt

Look at the verse in context. Think like a storyteller—how would you explain what's happening in your verse? Find the five senses in the story—sight, smell, sound, taste, and touch—as if you stepped into the characters' shoes. Look at what occurred before and after your verse. What's happening that caused the action in your verse?

Study Support Examples

Information you might find in your research . . .

Occasion and Purpose: "1. Luke's primary purpose is to strengthen and confirm the faith of the early Christians. He writes so that Theophilus (and other readers) "may know the certainty of the things" they have been taught (1:4). As for the exact "things" that require affirmation, one must look further into Luke's writing to find them."

"1:42 Blessed are you among women. This is a superlative, i.e., "Among all women, you are the most blessed" (cf. Judg 5:24).

1:43 my Lord. May allude to an important Messianic psalm: "The Lord says to my lord" (Ps 110:1; cf. Luke 20:41-44; Acts 2:34). **Lord.** An exalted Christological title in this context (cf. v. 76; 2:11; 4:12; 13:15, 35).

1:44 leaped for joy. This baby is able to experience joy even before his birth.

1:45 has believed. Mary's belief contrasts with Zechariah's disbelief (v. 20).

Excerpted from *NIV Biblical Theology Study Bible.* Copyright © 2015, 2018, Zondervan.

See how God takes the believed parts of every story and turns them into the fulfillment.

4 *actions* What actions develop the story in this verse? What is happening in this verse? To whom?

5 *outcome* _____

What is God saying to me today? How do I apply this to my life?

1 *verse* — What verse am I mapping? What key themes or specific words are speaking to me today?

2 *design* — — — — — — *develop* **3**

What different translations make up the design for this verse? Underline key phrases or words repeated.

What is the Hebrew or Greek meaning for the underlined phrases or words?

4 *actions*

What actions develop the story in this verse? What is happening in this verse? To whom?

5 *outcome*

What is God saying to me today? How do I apply this to my life?

1 *verse*   What verse am I mapping? What key themes or specific words are speaking to me today?

2 *design* ——————————— *develop* **3**

What different translations make up the design for this verse? Underline key phrases or words repeated.

What is the Hebrew or Greek meaning for the underlined phrases or words?

He Obeyed

*When all the people were being baptized, Jesus was baptized too.
And as he was praying, heaven was opened and the Holy Spirit
descended on him in bodily form like a dove. And a voice came from
heaven: "You are my Son, whom I love; with you I am well pleased."*

LUKE 3:21–22

OPENING REFLECTION

If we look around us, sacrifice isn't hidden away. It's there even in what we might see as insignificant moments. In the Gospel of Matthew, John the Baptist claims Jesus should be the one to baptize Him instead of the other way around. But the King steps back to place Himself behind those who'd lined up for baptism—those ready to embrace a new beginning with God are put before God in the flesh.

Jesus obeys, laying down His will and surrendering His all, to be the sacrifice for all.

The reminder of sacrifice and surrender begs a question from all of us: What if our schedule, our time, responsibilities, needs—even our desires and dreams—what if they all took a backseat to our relationship with God?

What kingdoms am I willing to give up in order to make Him King of my life?

GATHERING AND GETTING STARTED

Welcome back to session two of *Luke: Gathering the Goodness of God's Word*.

We've gathered for a second time—realizing there might have been sacrifice involved even in getting here today, or surrender in learning how to study in a new, in-depth, and possibly more vulnerable way.

To start, let's compare. After your first week verse mapping, discuss the following:

- *Compare and contrast the verse your group mapped. What did you discover through mapping the group verse? Where did your exploration take you?*

- *What verse(s) did you select to map on your own, and why? How did it go?*

- *What moments of faith-stretching did you experience in self-study time this week—did it take a step of faith to embrace a new approach to studying the Word?*

GATHERING: VIDEO STORY

Play the video segment for session two. As you watch the next installment of our Gospel of Luke story, follow the verse mapping guide points starting below and refer to the completed map on pages 42–43. Take brief notes or record questions that might lead you to further research in your independent study time this week.

Notes

1

What stands out in Luke 3:21–22:

> The act of sacrifice is to give of something we adore in this life—for a will and purpose greater than our own. God sacrificed for us, giving the world His Son, and Jesus sacrificed for the world, surrendering His will and offering His life.

The Gospels document Jesus' baptism, but Luke offers us the only clear indicator that the first thing Jesus did to embark upon ministry was to make Himself last. Instead of taking a step forward to lead and model obedience through being baptized FIRST, Jesus instead took a step back . . . to SACRIFICE and SURRENDER.

When we surrender to Jesus, we give back our lives—including the desire to hold onto the adored things of this life

② design

The word "when" in these verses indicates a place in time—meaning "just after"—establishing the FOUNDATION of faith through authentic sacrifice and surrender. Other translations of Luke 3:21–22 give the same indication that Jesus held back, placing Himself last by allowing others to be baptized before Him.

③ develop

In the Greek, "baptized" is *baptizó* (S. 907) [S. is an abbreviation for *The NIV Exhaustive Concordance*], meaning "to wash, baptize" or a ceremonial cleansing

In the Greek, "praying" is *proseuchomai* (S. 4336), meaning "to pray, earnestly, or most sincerely"

"Praying" is the present-tense form of the verb. It denotes action that is ongoing.

④ *actions*

Jesus is willing to SACRIFICE—making Himself last in servant leadership (Luke 3:21)

Jesus models SURRENDER in baptism—representing obedience to lay down His will, and the outward expression of His faith (Matthew 3:14–15; Mark 1:9–11; John 1:29–30)

Jesus seeks God first with PRAYER at a pivotal moment (Matthew 3:16; John 1:33)

Jesus further SURRENDERS to the sonship (and will of God) through the action of the Holy Spirit (Matthew 3:17; Mark 1:9–10)

5 *outcome*

To truly be set free from the enslavement of sin, we willingly make ourselves last. We SACRIFICE and SURRENDER—just as Jesus did for us.

What would it look like if we really needed the Word of God in a way that isn't a chore but a gift with every new day, and were willing to sacrifice to do what it says?

4  *What kingdoms am I willing to give up to make God the King of my life? What will I sacrifice? What will I surrender?*

The other Gospels (Matthew 3:13–17; Mark 1:9–11; John 1:29–34) also recorded accounts of Jesus' baptism, but Luke is the only one to document that the first thing Jesus did in ministry was to make Himself last

- **Jesus' acts of SACRIFICE:** *made Himself last in servant leadership* **(Luke 3:21)**

- **He models SURRENDER in baptism:** *represents obedience to lay down His will and the outward expression of His faith* **(Matthew 3:14–15; Mark 1:9–11; John 1:29–30)**

- **He seeks God first:** *PRAYER at a pivotal moment* **(Matthew 3:16; John 1:33)**

- **He further SURRENDERS** *to the Sonship (and will of God) through the action of the Holy Spirit* **(Matthew 3:17; Mark 1:9–10)**

5 *outcome* ——————————————————————

To truly be set free from the enslavement of sin, we willingly make ourselves last. We sacrifice and surrender.

1 *verse*   **LUKE 3:21–22 (NIV)**

"When all the people were being baptized, Jesus was baptized too. And as he was praying, heaven was opened and the Holy Spirit descended on him in bodily form like a dove. And a voice came from heaven: 'You are my Son, whom I love; with you I am well pleased.'"

2 *design* ———————————— *develop* **3**

- **NKJV:** *"When all the people were <u>baptized</u>, it came to pass that <u>Jesus also</u> was baptized; and while <u>He prayed</u>, the heaven was opened. . . ."*

- **BAPTIZED**—*baptizó (S. 907):*

  "to wash, baptize"; or a ceremonial cleansing

- **PRAYING**—*proseuchomai (S. 4336):*

  "to pray, earnestly, or most sincerely"

  Praying is the present tense form of the verb. It denotes action that is ongoing.

From the Video

I stepped off the hospital elevator and heard an unexpected but familiar comfort . . . music.

Someone was playing a dulcimer—the light, airy sound of strumming you can recognize almost without trying—a stringed melody of old-time hymns that I'd come to know so well. I'd bet the last thing the other patients expected to hear on that hospital floor was an impromptu concert coming from one of the patient rooms. But then, they didn't know my dad.

If they didn't know his heart belonged to Jesus, and to music, they soon would, just by walking down the hall. He was a member of a local dulcimer group, and they'd always played "I'll Fly Away" at the end of every performance. It didn't surprise me, then, to hear those notes drifting down the hall.

GATHERING: GROUP DISCUSSION

Take a few moments with your group to discuss the video you just watched and explore these concepts in Scripture.

1. What does it mean to be called a slave in the context of the world in which Jesus began His earthly ministry? (Think about slavery in first-century Rome.)

_____

_____

_____

2. Select a volunteer to read Romans 1:1–6 and Philippians 2:5–11 aloud to the group. Paul makes compelling statements about surrender, and how freedom is found in Christ Jesus alone. How is surrendering all to Jesus critical to our foundation of freedom in Him? How do we define "surrender" in our own lives?

_____

_____

_____

3. Select a volunteer(s) to read Matthew 3:14–15, Mark 1:9–11, and John 1:29–30 aloud to the group. How do these accounts of Jesus' baptism support His actions of sacrifice and surrender in Luke 3:21–22?

_____

_____

_____

4. From the start of Jesus' ministry, He models surrender to God's will for His life. List some results and obstacles we learn of sacrifice and surrender from His example?

_____

_____

_____

As you come to know Jesus better through verse mapping in the Gospel of Luke, what's one thing you need to surrender to Him by the time this study is over? Declare and discuss it. Pray over it. Then write it here, and expect God to move in the weeks ahead:

_____

_____

_____

GATHERING: GROUP ACTIVITY

For this activity, you will need a Bible, pens/markers, and a smart device (such as a phone or tablet).

- Using a Bible or Bible app on a smart device, look up two additional translations of Luke 3:21–22, and record them on the completed map on pages 42–43.

- To continue your verse mapping journey, pray as a group and <u>select one verse you'll map from Luke 3–4 in individual study time this week.</u> Gather in Week 3 and discuss how your map is the same or differed from others' maps.

GATHERING: CLOSING PRAYER

Jesus modeled prayer at pivotal moments in His faith journey—especially during times of sacrifice and surrender. In the same way, verse mapping can be a formative time in our relationship-building with Him. Mark this time with prayer today, gathering with open hearts, expecting the Holy Spirit to encourage you in areas you have yet to surrender, and to enrich the sacrifice of time you give to study the promises in His Word.

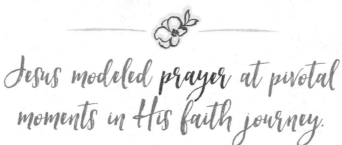

Jesus modeled prayer at pivotal moments in His faith journey.

INDIVIDUAL STUDY

He Obeyed

When all the people were being baptized, Jesus was baptized too. And as he was praying, heaven was opened and the Holy Spirit descended on him in bodily form like a dove. And a voice came from heaven: "You are my Son, whom I love; with you I am well pleased."

LUKE 3:21–22

The story of Jesus' baptism in Luke 3:21–22 establishes a foundation for how He would serve, sacricifice, and surrender to God in His ministry to come.

Remember that question we asked: What kingdoms am I willing to give up in order to make Him King of my life? It starts with taking an authentic look at what we're slaves to—and what we're willing to lay down in order to find freedom in Christ. Because what Jesus was born to do, and what He began in Luke 3:21–22, was to set the enslaved free.

GATHER: INDIVIDUAL STUDY INVITATION

This week, think about the symbolism of new life shown in baptism. The letting go of what doesn't need the cling of our hearts . . . the giving up of what doesn't offer freedom in God's Word . . . and the realization that what we find in Luke 3–4 is a Holy Spirit who is just as present in the peak moments of our journeys (3:21–22) as He is in the temptation and trials (4:1–13).

You're walking on this new-life journey now. Take a few more steps, a few more verses, a few more moments of breathing in the Word. The wilds are waiting.

Read
LUKE 3 — 4

Pray just before you go through these chapters. Whether it's five minutes today or an hour tomorrow, invite the Holy Spirit and gather with Him.

Read Luke 3–4. Focus in on the joy-moments. Shine a spotlight on those corners that need attention—those areas of our hearts that He's ready to champion if we'd only step back and let Him lead in our story. If your group selected a verse to map and discuss together, map that verse this week as well. Prepare to discuss what you've learned when your group gathers again.

Study Prompt

What gets lost in translation? How do the different translations present the same ideas or biblical principles?

The *design* identifies what the verse is calling attention to by comparing translations. The *design* calls out similar word choice, repetition of words, phrases, and/or aspects of grammar common across multiple translations. It brings to light what the verse is saying that cannot be lost to translation, and what may stand out as translation specific. Anything here could trigger a question or path for further investigation.

Study Support Examples

Information you might find in your research . . .

4:1–13 *Jesus Is Tested in the Wilderness.* Jesus' testing recalls Israel's experience in the wilderness (see note on Matt 4:1–11). Luke explicitly connects them by mentioning "wilderness" and "forty" (vv. 1–2; cf. Num 32:13; Deut 2:7; 29:5; Neh 9:21; Amos 2:10), since the "forty days" (v. 2) recalls Israel's "forty years" in the wilderness (Num 14:34). More important, all three OT passages that Jesus quotes in response to the devil come from Deut 6–8 (Deut 6:13 and Luke 4:8; Deut 6:16 and Luke 4:12, Deut 8:3 and Luke 4:4), a section that calls Israel to be faithful to God in the wilderness (Deut 6:16; 8:2). Moreover, the three specific temptations also parallel three significant instances in which Israel failed in the wilderness, and later traditions such as Ps 106 that recall Israel's faithlessness often point to these three events: (1) Israel failed to remember God in the way "they gave in to their craving" (Ps 106:14; cf. Exod 16:1–3; Num 11:1–6). (2) "They made a calf and worshiped an idol" (Ps 106:19; cf. Exod 32:1–15). (3) They tested and "rebelled against the Spirit of God" (Ps 106:33; cf. Exod 17:1–7; Num 20:1–13). Unlike Israel of old, Jesus the Son of God faithfully resists the devil's temptations.

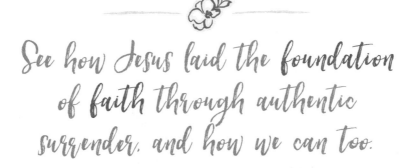

See how Jesus laid the foundation of faith through authentic surrender, and how we can too.

4 *actions*

What actions develop the story in this verse? What is happening in this verse? To whom?

5 *outcome*

What is God saying to me today? How do I apply this to my life?

1 *verse*   What verse am I mapping? What key themes or specific words are speaking to me today?

2 *design* ———————————— *develop* **3**

What different translations make up the design for this verse? Underline key phrases or words repeated.

What is the Hebrew or Greek meaning for the underlined phrases or words?

4 *actions*

What actions develop the story in this verse? What is happening in this verse? To whom?

5 *outcome* ─────────────────

What is God saying to me today? How do I apply this to my life?

1 *verse*   What verse am I mapping? What key themes or specific words are speaking to me today?

2 *design* ——————— *develop* **3**

What different translations make up the design for this verse? Underline key phrases or words repeated.

What is the Hebrew or Greek meaning for the underlined phrases or words?

⇒ *Washed Over* ⇐

*Then Jesus said to Simon, "Don't be afraid; from now
on you will fish for people." So they pulled their boats
up on shore, left everything and followed him.*

LUKE 5:10–11

OPENING REFLECTION

We probably don't feel like the disciple in Luke 5—the one who can drop nets and follow at a moment's notice. The fear that can hold us back from this kind of faith-walking is no cliché. It's raw, and real, and most times friction-causing.

Ever heard the acronym F.E.A.R. = False Evidence Appearing Real? There's some truth to how fear filters our sight through a lens of "what if?" worries. It drudges up past hurts. It illuminates present circumstances more than they deserve. And it tempts us with all the things we'd like to avoid in the future.

In these verses, Jesus calls us to step out. To follow Him in expectation. Without fear. Fully equipped to go wherever He asks. We take a hard look across the face of the deep this week, considering whether our biggest fears could be conquered by walking in the expectancy of what's to come instead of where we may fail and fall.

What gets in the way of the calling when we're "washed over" by the falling?

GATHERING AND GETTING STARTED

Welcome back for session three of *Luke: Gathering the Goodness of God's Word.*

We've gathered again, a couple of weeks into this verse mapping journey. But before we dive into today's story, we ask, "How's your heart?" After our first weeks in verse mapping, discuss the following in group share time:

- *Compare and contrast the verse your group mapped. What did you discover through mapping the group verse?*

- *What verse(s) did you select to map, and why?*

- *What moments of sacrifice and surrender did you encounter in your verse mapping self-study this week—were there impacts in carving out the time or confidence to do it? What tugged at a new space in your heart?*

GATHERING: VIDEO STORY

Play the video segment for session three. As you watch the next installment of our Gospel of Luke story, follow the verse mapping guide points starting below and refer to the completed map on pages 60–61. Take brief notes or record questions that might lead you to further research in your independent study time this week.

Notes

1

What stands out in Luke 5:10–11:

> If we're not careful, fear can take us to a place of doubt-living instead of promise-believing

Jesus very clearly calls us to let down our nets with expectancy, believing God will bring in a catch once we follow Him out of shallow waters—and have nothing to fear when we do

2 design

Jesus says, "Fear not; from henceforth thou shalt catch men" (KJV)

The New King James Version: "So when [meaning "just after"] they had brought their boats to land, they forsook all and followed Him."

Other translations: "'There is nothing to fear.' . . . They pulled their boats up on the beach, left them, nets and all, and followed him" (MSG). And, "'Do not fear, from now on you will be catching men.' When they had brought their boats to land, they left everything and followed Him" (NASB).

③ develop

Throughout the Gospel of Luke, there are three Greek words to describe fear: *phobos* (S. 5401), *phobeó* (S. 5399), and *aphobós* (S. 870)

In the Greek, *phobos* and *phobeó* have similar definitions, meaning "fear, dread, or terror; and reverence." (Remember the origin of the word "phobia.")

In the Greek, *aphobós* means "without fear" or "fearlessly." It's the complete opposite of doubt-living; it's promise-seeking.

When fear arrives, faith fades

④ actions

James and John were in the boat but left everything and followed Jesus (Matthew 4:18–22; Mark 1:16–20)

The disciples embraced what Jesus said: be fearLESS and follow with expectancy (v. 11)

Jesus tells Simon "don't be afraid" (v. 10); "fear not" in other translations (S. 5399): means "terror or dread" (or "reverence"). In the definition is an action: the Greek word means "to flee."

5 *outcome*

When the storms of life come our way, fear can cause us to turn away and flee. Instead, we stay in the boat and draw near to Jesus, knowing it's in the stormy, upon-the-deep moments we need Him the most.

Find your courage to drop nets and venture out into the deep—knowing that we need never fear the falling because He's already equipped us for our calling.

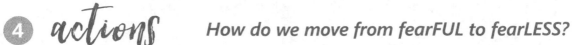

4 *actions*   **How do we move from fearFUL to fearLESS?**

Expectancy: *Disciples heard Jesus' call and EXPECTED something to happen if they followed Jesus:*

- *James and John* **(Matthew 4:18–22; Mark 1:16–20)** *were IN THE BOAT with their father. Left everything and followed Jesus.*

- *The disciples embraced what Jesus had said: be fearLESS and follow with expectancy* **(v. 11)**

- *Jesus tells Simon "don't be afraid" in* **verse 10**—*also, "fear not" in other translations (S. 5399)—means "terror or dread" (also, "reverence").*

- *Buried in the definition is also an ACTION . . . the Greek word means "to flee."*

5 *outcome*

When the storms of life come our way, fear can cause us to turn away from Him and flee. But instead, we stay in the boat and draw near to Jesus . . . knowing it's in the stormy moments we need Him the most.

1 *verse* **LUKE 5:10–11 (NIV)**

"Then Jesus said to Simon, 'Don't be afraid; from now on you will fish for people.' So they pulled their boats up on shore, left everything and followed him."

2 *design* ——————————— *develop* **3**

- **NKJV:** *"And Jesus said to Simon, 'Do not be <u>afraid</u>. From now on you will catch men.' So when they had brought their boats to land, they forsook all and followed Him."*

- **FEAR**—*phobos (S. 5401); phobeó (S. 5399):*

  "fear, dread or terror; and reverence"

- **FEAR**—*aphobós (S. 870):*

  "without fear," or, "fearlessly"

- **F.E.A.R.** = *False Evidence Appearing Real*

- *When fear arrives, faith fades.*

▶▶ From the Video ◀◀

My husband and I sent our sons to their rooms one evening so we could have one of those "adult conversations"—the important kind you know has the potential to change everything. Dinner was forgotten—bubbling away on the stove. We just stood in the kitchen. Arms around each other. My husband nudged his chin against the top of my head. And listened.

He didn't interrupt as I wept words, outlining a somewhat irrational plan to upend our family, abandon security . . . and walk away from the career I'd spent a decade and a half in building.

After that day in the office when I'd heard the heart-whisper "your time at this company is done," another year had flown by. And I hadn't stepped out. I hadn't done anything, really, except bury the growing weight of that calling further down inside me. I couldn't shake the feeling that I'd regret it if I didn't at least try to step out and follow what was on my heart. But it wasn't just me. It would require that WE walk away from all we'd known as a family—all five of us—and instead choose a different story.

GATHERING: GROUP DISCUSSION

Take a few moments with your group to discuss the video you just watched and explore these concepts in Scripture.

1. Think about the context of the disciples' task to overcome their fears and trust Jesus enough to first let down their nets on the Sea of Galilee, then to head out into the deep with Him. What are the possible consequences for their livelihood, protection, and provision if they follow Him? What are the consequences if they don't?

_____

_____

_____

2. Select a volunteer (or more than one) to read Matthew 4:18–22, Mark 1:16–20, and Luke 5:1–11 aloud to the group. Here Jesus calls four fishermen to be disciples, and they immediately dropped their nets to follow Him. How do we go from a believer who was once fearFUL just steps from shore to a disciple who is fearLESS and faithful, even when we launch out into the deep?

----

3. In today's video story, Kristy talked about not wanting to lose any more time on the wrong journey, and how her family's "dropping-nets" experience radically changed how they chose to follow Jesus. When can the fear of *not* following Jesus overcome the smaller fears that may try to keep us from stepping out with Him?

SESSION 3

4. Why would Jesus call fishermen to be disciples? By religous standards of the day, they were hardly equipped to follow Him as "fishers of men." Discuss real-world ways Jesus uses us today, even if we don't appear equipped for the task ahead.

What does being equipped mean to you?

How does faith in Jesus redefine what it means to be equipped?

_____

_____

_____

GATHERING: GROUP ACTIVITY

For this activity, you will need a Bible, pens/markers, and a smart device (such as a phone or tablet).

- Using a Bible or Bible app on a smart device, look up two additional translations of Luke 5:10–11, and record them on the completed map on pages 60–61.

- To continue your verse mapping journey, pray as a group and <u>select one verse you'll map from Luke 5–10 in individual study time this week.</u> Gather in Week 4 and discuss how your map is the same or differed from others' maps.

GATHERING: CLOSING PRAYER

Jesus' calling of the disciples reminds us what fear can do: when the storms of life come our way, they may cause us to turn away from Him and flee.

Today we pray to stay in the boat. We pray to draw near to Jesus, knowing it's in the stormy moments we need Him the most. And in spite of our fears, we'll still drop nets into the water, head out into the deep, and journey with Him.

Today we pray to stay in the boat.

INDIVIDUAL STUDY

Washed Over

Then Jesus said to Simon, "Don't be afraid; from now on you will fish for people." So they pulled their boats up on shore, left everything and followed him.

LUKE 5:10–11

Our journey with Jesus is not determined by our definition of "equipped," and it certainly doesn't have to be derailed by our host of fears.

Either we trust, or we don't. Either we let our nets into the water, or they stay in the boat. That's the opportunity Jesus offers in Luke 5:10–11. But we also see that if we're faithful to Him and trust to go a little ways from shore, He'll be faithful in return. And then He'll ask it of us again. "Now go a little further . . . just a little more . . . and a little more . . ." until we're in the deep, trusting, and fully dependent upon Him.

What gets in the way of the calling when we're "washed over" by the falling?

GATHER: INDIVIDUAL STUDY INVITATION

Fishermen. Lepers. Tax collectors. Apostles and sinners. You find them all in Luke 5–10.

In fact, you may find yourself as you map these verses. You may see the redemption and taste the saltiness of healing tears that fall down. You may feel renewed empathy for the poor and hungry—because "blessed are they" say the Beatitudes (6:20–26). You may feel the sting of conviction or understanding in the parables (8:4–18). You'll marvel at the absolute majesty of a Savior who can command the wind and waves to be at peace (8:22–25), even though they threaten to wash you over.

Jesus told stories. Let that sink in, because you're learning and mapping and walking with Him, and the only way He does it is above the waves.

Read

LUKE 5 – 10

Pray and determine where you'll spend time with the Holy Spirit in Luke 5–10. You can study chronologically (reading through the early chapters of Jesus' ministry and mapping interactions with the people and teaching to the disciples), or stay on theme with the topic of fear.

Read Luke 5–10, gathering with the Holy Spirit. If you want to stay on theme with conquering fears and walking with expectancy, a good section to map may be Luke 8:22–25. If your group selected a verse to map and discuss together, map that verse this week as well. Prepare to discuss what you've learned when your group gathers again.

Study Prompt

Actions record:

- What's happening in the verse

- Who the characters are in what you're reading

- How their story relates to other stories/verses/persons in other areas of Scripture

- What are the topics, themes, dates of significant events, and/or theological elements of the verse(s) you're researching

Study Support Examples

Information you might find in your research . . .

5:10 James and John. Along with Peter, they form the core of Jesus' group of disciples (8:51; 9:28). **fish for people.** Unlike the act of fishing where the goal is capturing and killing fish, these disciples are called to give life to people through the proclamation of the gospel.

9:1–9 *Jesus Sends Out the Twelve.* Jesus commissions the 12 disciples that he had appointed (6:12–16). As Jesus was able to cast out demons (8:26–39) and cure diseases (8:40–56), the 12 disciples now receive power to continue Jesus' ministry by performing the same miracles (v. 1). As Jesus was rejected by his own people (4:14–30; cf. 7:30–35), these disciples will also suffer the same fate (v. 5). Herod's question concerning Jesus' identity (vv. 7–9) anticipates vv. 18–27.

In 1986, a first-century boat was unearthed from the Sea of Galilee. While there are no direct links to the Gospel stories, it is a good representation of what a generic Sea of Galilee fishing boat looked like in the first century.

Excerpted from *NIV Theology Study Bible.* Copyright © 2015, 2018, Zondervan.

SESSION 3

4 *actions*   What actions develop the story in this verse? What is happening in this verse? To whom?

5 *outcome* _____

What is God saying to me today? How do I apply this to my life?

1 *verse*   What verse am I mapping? What key themes or specific words are speaking to me today?

2 *design* ———————— *develop* **3**

What different  translations make up the design for this verse? Underline key phrases or words repeated.

What is the Hebrew or Greek meaning for the underlined phrases or words?

4 *actions*

What actions develop the story in this verse? What is happening in this verse? To whom?

5 *outcome*

What is God saying to me today? How do I apply this to my life?

1  What verse am I mapping? What key themes or specific words are speaking to me today?

2 *design* ———————— *develop* **3**

What different translations make up the design for this verse? Underline key phrases or words repeated.

What is the Hebrew or Greek meaning for the underlined phrases or words?

session 4

Restored

*"So I say to you: Ask and it will be given to you; seek and
you will find; knock and the door will be opened to you.
For everyone who asks receives; the one who seeks finds;
and to the one who knocks, the door will be opened."*

LUKE 11:9–10

OPENING REFLECTION

This was where the disciples—twelve called and chosen men—would find themselves as they traveled ministry roads with Jesus. And this is their promise of restoration. They would see how He's patient as we learn. Grace-filled as we fumble and fall. And they'd experience firsthand that we're not as lost as we may have thought.

We are REDEEMED in Jesus Christ. For the past, present, and future versions of ourselves—no matter where the failures or faults in how we navigate winding roads, He walks alongside us.

What if our restoration—past, present, and future—is just a knock away?

GATHERING AND GETTING STARTED

Welcome back for session four of *Luke: Gathering the Goodness of God's Word.*

We've gathered at the halfway point of our mapping journey—having encountered Jesus in the areas of our FAITH and FOUNDATION, our FEARS, and this week, our FAILURES.

How has your time with the Holy Spirit encouraged your heart? Share some defining moments or thoughts about your verse mapping journey in the Gospel of Luke so far.

- *Compare and contrast the verse your group mapped. Can you identify a common thread or truth that was revealed in everyone's map of the same verse?*

- *What fears did you encounter in your personal verse mapping this past week—were there any distractions or obstacles that impacted your time or confidence to do it? Share what verse(s) you mapped.*

- *Share any specific areas in which you were you able to "drop nets" and trust Jesus in a deeper way.*

GATHERING: VIDEO STORY

Play the video segment for session four. As you watch the next installment of our Gospel of Luke story, follow the verse mapping guide points starting below and refer to the completed map on pages 78–79. Take brief notes or record questions that might lead you to further research in your independent study time this week.

Notes

1 *verse*

What stands out in these verses:

> By Luke 11, the disciples are committed to day-by-day ministry with Jesus, watching Him pray at pivotal moments—during His baptism (Luke 3:21), when He called them into ministry (Luke 6:12), and when He outlined a model prayer (Luke 11:2–4)

Jesus' instructions are to ask and we'll receive, seek and we'll find, knock and the door will be opened—but we ask with faith, and trust that we'll receive

Jesus provides firm guidance on how to stay in step with God in our day-by-day journeys, and in the times we may be lost in our own failure. We have the opportunity to pray and seek restoration with God, even before we know we need it.

② design

Jesus tells us we'll stay close in the day-by-day if we ask, seek, and knock (NKJV)

Other translations mirror the promises in these same three actions: "Ask and you'll get; seek and you'll find; knock and the door will open" (MSG). "Ask, and it will be given to you; seek, and you will find; knock, and it will be opened to you" (NASB).

③ develop

In the Greek, *aiteó* (S. 154) means "to ask, request, or petition to the point of begging"—even "calling out" to

In the Greek, *zéteó* (S. 2212) means "to search for or desire; to investigate, in order to reach a binding (or, final) resolution"; and to "keep trying to obtain"

In the Greek, *krouó* (S. 2925) means "to knock"

4 actions

Jesus frequently takes time away to ASK, SEEK, and KNOCK—modeled at pivotal times:

- In prayer during Jesus' baptism (Luke 3:21–22)

- In prayer for the selection of the twelve disciples (Luke 6:12–13)

- When the disciples question how to SEEK God, He outlines the model prayer (Luke 11:1–4)

- When preaching on SEEKING a sign—through faith (Luke 11:29–33)

- He SEEKS God through intense prayer prior to His crucifixion (Luke 22:39–44)

5 *outcome*

We keep asking; we pray, pray, PRAY. And we don't stop SEEKING Him, especially when circumstances are good. And when we KNOCK . . . we're patient, remembering His timing is not our own.

> My failure in one area brought us to God's absolute majesty in another.

4  *What if our restoration from our FAILURES— past, present, and future—is just a knock away?*

Jesus frequently takes time away to ASK, SEEK, and KNOCK—modeled at pivotal times:

- *In prayer during Jesus' baptism (**Luke 3:21–22**)*

- *In prayer for selection of the twelve disciples (**Luke 6:12–13**)*

- *When disciples question how to SEEK God, Jesus outlines the model prayer (**Luke 11:1–4**)*

- *Jesus preaches on SEEKING a sign—through faith (**Luke 11:29–33**)*

- *He SEEKS God through intense prayer (**Luke 22:39–44**)*

Jesus' instructions are to ask and we'll receive, seek and we'll find, knock and the door will be opened—but we ask with faith, and trust that we'll receive.

5 *outcome* ─────────────

We keep asking; we pray, pray, PRAY. And we don't stop SEEKING Him, especially when circumstances are good. And when we KNOCK . . . we're patient, remembering His timing is not our own.

1 *verse*   **LUKE 11:9–10 (NIV)**

"So I say to you: <u>Ask</u> and it will be given to you; <u>seek</u> and you will find; <u>knock</u> and the door will be opened to you. For everyone who asks receives; the one who seeks finds; and to the one who knocks, the door will be opened."

2 *design* ———————— *develop* **3**

- **NKJV:** *"So I say to you, <u>ask</u>, and it will be given to you; <u>seek</u>, and you will find; <u>knock</u>, and it will be opened to you. For everyone who asks receives, and he who seeks finds, and to him who knocks it will be opened."*

- **ASK**—*aiteó (S. 154):*

  "to ask, request, or petition to the point of begging"—even "calling out to"

- **SEEK**—*zéteó (S. 2212)*

  "to search for or desire; to investigate, in order to reach a binding (or, final) resolution"; and to "keep trying to obtain"

- **KNOCK**—*krouó (S. 2925)*

  "to knock; to beat the door to gain admittance"

SESSION 4

From the Video

My husband and I loaded into our tiny rental car and set out on a nine-day road trip through the back roads of Ireland. We'd brought our oldest sons along. It seemed that nothing would hinder our exploration of the unknown. We walked down roads lined with rock walls and cottages dotting green hills. We toured castle ruins, hiked through the woods, and stopped to do book research in tucked-away towns.

On that day, my husband handed me the map. It would be his job to brave the country roads—driving on the opposite side of the car and on the unfamiliar side of the road—and get us to our inn by evening. It was my job to take the map and navigate how we were going to go about it.

It turns out that my failure in one area—reading maps—had brought us to God's absolute majesty in another. It had been a tough season, but with brilliant, rainbow bookends. And all I could think as we stood there together, with no words—just snapping photos, smiling, and staring out at sea and cliffs and a colored sky—was that we were restored in the one way God knew we needed.

GATHERING: GROUP DISCUSSION

Take a few moments with your group to discuss the video you just watched and explore these concepts in Scripture.

1. Think about all that the disciples have witnessed of Jesus' ministry from being called and chosen in Luke 6:13 through this week's verses in Luke 11. The disciples are present as Jesus preaches the Beatitudes (6:20–23). They listen to parables, like those of the Sower (7:4–18) and the Good Samaritan (10:25–37). They witness Jesus perform both miracles (9:16–17) and healings (6:17; 8:40–48), and marvel as He displays authority over the elements, calming the wind and waves on a stormy sea (8:24–25). After everything they've

witnessed, how could they still struggle with knowing how to pray? Is our daily communion with God dependent on more than what we see or do?

_____

_____

_____

2. Select a volunteer to read Luke 11:1–8 and 22:39–44. How do these passages present a link between prayer, faith, and restoration? At what other pivotal moments does Jesus stop and step away to pray?

_____

_____

_____

3. Jesus says "*everyone who asks receives*" (v. 10). When we petition God through prayer, why is our answer sometimes not what we asked for? Can this statement still be true if God's answer is *no*?

_____

_____

_____

4. The Greek word *zéteó* (S. 2212) means "to search for or desire; to investigate, in order to reach a binding (or, final) resolution"; and to "keep trying to obtain." Discuss ways we keep trying to obtain a relationship with God. If we seek God through study of His Word, is that enough to obtain a close walk with Him?

_____

_____

_____

Define "restored." If there is an area where you long for restoration, what is it?

_____

_____

_____

GATHERING: GROUP ACTIVITY

For this activity, you will need a Bible, pens/markers, and a smart device (such as a phone or tablet).

- Using a Bible or Bible app on a smart device, look up two additional translations of Luke 11:9–10, and record them on the completed map on pages 78–79.

- To continue your verse mapping journey, pray as a group and <u>select one verse from Luke 11–14 you'll map in individual study time this week.</u> Gather in Week 5 and discuss how your map is the same or differed from others' maps.

GATHERING: CLOSING PRAYER

Jesus tells us, in plain words: ASK, SEEK, and KNOCK.

Today we pray that our voice would whisper His name, our hearts would seek His Word, and our hands would be open to receive what He's promised. Whether trekking unfamiliar roads or walking joy-filled paths, we pray our steps would stay in stride with Him.

We pray our steps would stay in stride with Him.

session 4

INDIVIDUAL STUDY

Restored

"So I say to you: Ask and it will be given to you; seek and you will find; knock and the door will be opened to you. For everyone who asks receives; the one who seeks finds; and to the one who knocks, the door will be opened."

LUKE 11:9–10

Through the peaks or valley-walking, or navigating those winding back roads of a new journey, Jesus offers authentic rest and restoration if we ASK, SEEK, and KNOCK every day.

GATHER: INDIVIDUAL STUDY INVITATION

This week, you're going on a journey in Luke 11–14. Keep going. Keep walking. Keep learning essentials like the model prayer (11:1–4). You're going to be asking, seeking, and knocking as your pen flies over the pages (11:9–13). You're going to be told not to worry (12:22), to cultivate faith as tiny as a mustard seed (13:18–19), and to walk the narrow way through the gate that brings life (13:22–24).

In each story, there's restoration for the exact place you are today—and Jesus meets you there. Embrace the Savior who wants to be real in your life every day.

If you want to develop a habit of time with God in the day-by-day, a great place to start this week may be the Lord's Prayer (Luke 11:1–4). You might find that to really seek and knock, you have to first know how to ask—just as Jesus did, in the everyday and in the pivotal moments—and that comes from knowing how to pray.

Read

LUKE 11 – 14

Pray. Sit in His presence. Lean back in your chair. Look up at the glorious landscape and rainbow-colored sky. Gather with Him . . . and listen to what He has to say.

Read Luke 11–14. Time spent verse mapping will draw us closer to Him in every season of our faith walk. Take time this week to ASK by giving prayer the priority over a packed schedule. SEEK—scoot over and offer Him the driver's seat on your verse mapping journey. And KNOCK, knowing it doesn't always require your knuckles hitting the door for it to open.

Study Prompt

The *outcome* is a quick-hit summary of what you've learned. One or two sentences should do it. Summarize, jot it down, and come back later to find where the Holy Spirit has confirmed His promises to you. This is your claim on this verse, at this time of your life. The *outcome* should reflect whatever truth has been revealed in your map.

Study Support Examples

Information you might find in your research . . .

A. Journey to Jerusalem (9:51–19:44)

B. Call to Repentance in the Midst of Opposition (11:14–13:35)

  1. Jesus and Beelzebul (11:14–28)

  2. The Sign of Jonah (11:29–32)

  3. The Lamp of the Body (11:33–36)

  4. Woes on the Pharisees and the Experts in the Law (11:37–54)

  5. Warning and Encouagements (12:1–12)

  6. The Parable of the Rich Fool (12:13–21)

  7. Do Not Worry (12:22–34)

  8. Watchfulness (12:35–48)

  9. Not Peace but Division (12:49–53)

  10. Interpreting the Times (12:54–59)

  11. Repent or Perish (13:1–35)

  12. Jesus Heals a Crippled Woman on the Sabbath (13:10–17)

  13. The Parables of the Mustard Seed and the Yeast (13:18–21)

  14. The Narrow Door (13:22–30)

  15. Jesus' Sorrow for Jerusalem (13:31–35)

Excerpted from *NIV Theology Study Bible*.
Copyright © 2015, 2018, Zondervan.

Steps to the Pool of Siloam were discovered in Jerusalem in 2004

4 *actions*

What actions develop the story in this verse? What is happening in this verse? To whom?

5 *outcome*

What is God saying to me today? How do I apply this to my life?

1 *verse*   What verse am I mapping? What key themes or specific words are speaking to me today?

2 *design* ———————————— *develop* **3**

What different translations make up the design for this verse? Underline key phrases or words repeated.

What is the Hebrew or Greek meaning for the underlined phrases or words?

4 *actions*   What actions develop the story in this verse? What is happening in this verse? To whom?

5 *outcome* ————————————————————

What is God saying to me today? How do I apply this to my life?

1 *verse*   What verse am I mapping? What key themes or specific words are speaking to me today?

2 *design* ———————————— *develop* **3**

What different  translations make up the design for this verse? Underline key phrases or words repeated.

What is the Hebrew or Greek meaning for the underlined phrases or words?

The Cry

"If anyone comes to me and does not hate father and mother, wife and children, brothers and sisters—yes, even their own life—such a person cannot be my disciple. And whoever does not carry their cross and follow me cannot be my disciple."

LUKE 14:26–27

Jesus called out with a loud voice, "Father, into your hands I commit my spirit." When he had said this, he breathed his last.

LUKE 23:46

OPENING REFLECTION

What is the cost of discipleship? In these verses, we have the opportunity to consider the deep commitment this question poses for each of us—whether it's in the joy-filled moments or the darkest of circumstances of our lives. Jesus says we carry our cross.

This week is firmly rooted in Jesus' bold cry, and the bold love He has for us (Luke 23:46). This is the story of a Savior. And a cross. And the beautiful commitment He made, where the cost was us.

What if our commitment was so strong that we came each time He called?

GATHERING AND GETTING STARTED

Welcome back for session five of *Luke: Gathering the Goodness of God's Word.*

Now that we're becoming experienced mappers in the Gospel of Luke, we gather this week to consider the cost and commitment of discipleship. Where did verse mapping Luke 11–14 take you this week? Discuss your journey with your group.

- *Compare and contrast the verse your group mapped. Are there any noticeable patterns developing in focus or similarities/differences in mapping the group verse?*

- *What verse(s) did you select to map, and why? How did it go?*

- *In what areas of your daily walk were you encouraged this week? Were you able to ASK, make time to SEEK, and KNOCK, expecting the Holy Spirit to meet you where you were?*

GATHERING: VIDEO STORY

Play the video segment for session five. As you watch the next installment of our Gospel of Luke story, follow the verse mapping guide points starting below and refer to the completed map on pages 96–97. Take brief notes or record questions that might lead you to further research in your independent study time this week.

Notes

1 *Verse*

What stands out in these verses:

> In Luke 14:26, Jesus turns to the crowd and says: "If anyone comes to me and does not hate father and mother, wife and children, brothers and sisters—yes, even their own life—such a person cannot be my disciple"

Jesus makes a bold statement about the cost required to truly surrender all and follow Him. To consider the cost of discipleship, we must understand what the requirement holds.

We CARRY our cross. Jesus uses the present tense, indicating our surrender to Him is an active commitment—in the right now, and every day in our future.

❷ design

"And whoever does not CARRY THEIR CROSS and FOLLOW ME cannot be my DISCIPLE" (Luke 14:27 NIV).

"And whosoever doth not BEAR HIS CROSS, and COME AFTER ME, cannot be My DISCIPLE" (KJV).

Other translations echo the similar, strong language: "Anyone who won't shoulder his own cross and follow behind me can't be my disciple" (MSG). "Whoever does not carry his own cross and come after Me cannot be My disciple" (NASB).

③ *develop*

In the Greek, *bastazó* (S. 941) means "to carry away, to bear." Within the root meaning, this carrying is to "tolerate or endure," even going so far as to indicate enduring hardships. As a symbol of execution, there's nothing greater to endure than the cross.

In the Greek, *mathétés* (S. 3101) means "a student; a learner or ardent follower." This is the same word Jesus uses in the New Testament to refer to His twelve disciples. His meaning is clear: in order to be called a disciple of Christ, nothing can come before our commitment to Him.

In the Greek, *phóneó* (S. 5455) means "to call out, or summon." Jesus carried the cross for us and He cries out, summoning the Father to carry it for Him.

④ *actions*

To consider the cost of following Christ:

"If anyone comes to me and does not hate father and mother, wife and children, brothers and sisters—yes, even their own life—such a person cannot be my disciple" (v. 26)—we must have *no one* who comes before Jesus in our lives

"Those of you who do not give up everything you have cannot be my disciples" (v. 33)—
we must have *nothing* that comes before Jesus in our lives

Jesus is asking us to give up everything we have for Him—just as He gives up everything
for us (Luke 23:46)

 ⑤ outcome

Our commitment to Jesus is so strong—we consider the cost and take up our cross . . .
nothing comes before Jesus in the disciple's heart

> *"In the same way, those of you*
> *who do not give up everything*
> *you have cannot be my disciples."*
> *(LUKE 14:33)*

 **4** *actions*

What is our commitment to follow Jesus—do we consider the cost of discipleship, and can we take up that cross?

Jesus is clear—we need to consider the cost of following Him:

- *"If anyone comes to me and does not hate father and mother, wife and children, brothers and sisters—yes, even their own life—such a person cannot be my disciple . . ."* **(v. 26)**—*We have* **no one** *who comes before Jesus in our lives.*

- *". . . those of you who do not give up everything you have cannot be my disciples . . ."* **(v. 33)**—*We have* **nothing** *that comes before Jesus in our lives.*

Jesus is asking us to give up everything we have for Him—just as He gives up everything for us. **(Luke 23:46)**

 **5** *outcome*

Our commitment to Jesus is so strong—we consider the cost, and take up our cross. . . . Nothing comes before Jesus in the disciple's heart.

① *verse*   **LUKE 14:27 / 23:46 (NIV)**

"And whoever does not <u>carry</u> their cross and follow me cannot be my <u>disciple</u>."

"Jesus <u>called out</u> with a loud voice, 'Father, into your hands I commit my spirit.' When he had said this, he breathed his last."

② *design* ——— *develop* ③

- **NKJV:** *"And whoever does not bear his cross and come after Me cannot be My disciple."*

- **CARRY**—*bastazó (S. 941):*

   "to carry away, to bear" and *"to tolerate or endure through hardship"*

   The verb is in present tense—this denotes action that is ongoing, and without end

- **DISCIPLE**—*mathétés (S. 3101):*

   "a student; a learner or ardent follower"

- **CALLED OUT**—*phóneó (S. 5455):*
   "to call out, or summon"

SESSION 5

◄ From the Video ►

I found a seat and settled in the back of the history class—never expecting that day would change my life. The professor dimmed the lights, and we art students readied our pens to take notes on famous twentieth-century artists like Pablo Picasso, Claude Monet, and Henri Matisse. So we were ready when slide images began to cut the darkness and paint the front wall of our classroom with color and light.

Before us were watercolor landscapes by artists we didn't know. There were images of flowers and butterflies. Clouds, sky, and sun. There were portraits, some expert drawings by a trained hand; others, cut paper with poetry and music notes. The art started out as these softer things—some even painted by a child's hand. But then the mood shifted. The images became more menacing in nature. There was a subdued darkness in the pencil and charcoal portraits of people owning sad eyes and stark faces. There were guards with guns. Watchtowers. Barbed wire and prisoners in striped uniforms. And long trains of cattle cars packed with people.

This was the art *of* the Holocaust—images created by prisoners from *inside* the barbed wire fences of concentration camps. Suddenly, the air shifted in the classroom. We were stunned. Silence was our response.

As I looked at the paintings by these prisoners, I realized they'd considered the cost . . . and found it worthy enough to surrender all they had to use the gifts God had placed on their hearts.

 This is the story of a Savior. And a cross.

GATHERING: GROUP DISCUSSION

Take a few moments with your group to discuss the video you just watched and explore these concepts in Scripture.

1. Think about the meaning of "disciple" in the context of Hebrew culture. How does Jesus challenge the preconceived idea that discipleship is limited to an elite few, instead inviting all to become students of righteousness? Is there a difference in being called a believer and living as a disciple?

   _____

   _____

   _____

2. Select a volunteer (or more than one) to read Luke 14:28–33 and Luke 23:44–49 aloud to the group. Jesus is clear about the cost of discipleship—both in word and in action. What does He ask us to surrender in order to follow Him? Go around the group and share something you've given up—or would surrender—for something or someone dear to you.

   _____

   _____

   _____

3. The Greek for "carry" is *bastazó* (S. 941), meaning "to carry away, to bear." Can bearing burdens ever be a good thing? How can the enduring of hardships or carrying burdens be used by God?

   _____

   _____

   _____

What does discipleship mean to you?

_____

_____

If you had to give up everything to follow Jesus, what would be *one thing* that could have the potential to hold you back?

_____

_____

GATHERING: GROUP ACTIVITY

For this activity, each participant will need a Bible, pens/markers, and a smart device (such as a phone or tablet).

● Using a Bible or Bible app on a smart device, look up two additional translations of Luke 14:27 or 23:46, and record them on the completed map on pages 96–97.

● To continue your verse mapping journey, pray as a group and select one verse you'll map from Luke 15–23 in individual study time this week. Gather in Week 6 and discuss how your map is the same or differed from others' maps.

GATHERING: CLOSING PRAYER

When we picture Jesus shouldering a cross on the way to His crucifixion we realize the great debt He paid for us. Today, we pray that we would bear every cross for Him. We pray that nothing would come between us and our ability to follow Jesus as a true disciple—an ardent follower and lifelong student of righteousness.

session 5

INDIVIDUAL STUDY

The Cry

"If anyone comes to me and does not hate father and mother, wife and children, brothers and sisters—yes, even their own life—such a person cannot be my disciple. And whoever does not carry their cross and follow me cannot be my disciple."

LUKE 14:26–27

Jesus called out with a loud voice, "Father, into your hands I commit my spirit." When he had said this, he breathed his last.

LUKE 23:46

You may have been a mere believer once, but today you know you're more. You have the spiritual eyes to see and taste and experience life as a disciple of Jesus Christ in Luke 15–23, and there's no going back.

You're an heir instead of orphaned (15:1–7), a son or daughter instead of a prodigal (15:11–31), and a doer of all things impossible for human beings but possible with God (18:26–27). There's triumph (19:28–38) and tragedy to come (21:20–24), and the King who dies with your name on His lips (23:44–49) . . . but that's only where your story begins.

GATHER: INDIVIDUAL STUDY INVITATION

As we open the final chapters leading to Jesus' cry from the cross, we begin to really see Him—maybe for that authentic first time—as the loving focal point of the most important relationship we will ever have. You will read of the teaching, the healings, the final moments with His disciples, and the exquisite portrait of His grace.

Take the opportunity to become a lifelong learner. A student of righteousness. And a follower of His example.

This week? It's a rocky road to the cross.

Next week? We celebrate restoration and the eternal promise that redemption reigns, and He lives in us.

Read

⇒ LUKE 15 — 23 ⇐

Pray. We are deep in the GATHERING. Jesus has summoned us and we're shouldering our cross day by day. Whether it's five minutes today or an hour tomorrow, invite the Holy Spirit and gather with Him. Seek God's face in the verse(s) you will map this week.

Read Luke 15–23. Consider the times when you (or areas of your life) have been lost. Open your hands from the things you have clenched and held tightly to. Be honest about your priorities and with whom in these chapters you relate to most. If your group selected a verse to map and discuss together, map that verse this week as well. Prepare to discuss what you've learned when your group gathers again.

Let the Holy Spirit reveal to you the hope and security and satisfaction available in Jesus Christ.

Next week we will focus on GOING into the world to share what we know and make followers and lovers of Jesus Christ.

During our final week, you will do two things:

- **Take action.** Develop a mapping plan for individual study—STEP OUT on a new story road in order to STEP IN to your calling with Him.

- **Make your own commitment.** Sign on the "dotted line" of your heart that the Word of God will be primary in your life, and let your life be changed eternally through discipleship with Jesus.

Study Prompt

What verse are you mapping? What key themes or specific words are speaking to you today?

- *What's on your heart today?* If you're facing a difficult circumstance, or find yourself in an unexpected path in your own story with God, select a verse(s) that speaks to the theme of your heart for today.

- *What's that word?* If you're reading Scripture and something jumps off the page—a word you don't recognize, a city you've never heard of, or a phrase you don't quite understand—this is a good indication it might be your verse(s) to map for the day.

Let the Holy Spirit reveal to you the hope and security and satisfaction available in Jesus Christ.

Study Support Examples

Information you might find in your research . . .

⑈ PARABLES OF JESUS ⑈

Parable	Matthew	Mark	Luke
Lamp under a bowl	5:14–15	4:21–22	8:16; 11:33
Wise and foolish builders	7:24–27		6:47–49
New cloth on an old garment	9:16	2:21	5:36
New wine in old sheepskins	9:17	2:22	5:37–39
Sower and the soils	13:3–8, 18–23	4:3–8, 14–20	8:5–8, 11–15
Weeds	13:24–30, 36–43		
Mustard seed	13:31–32	4:30–32	13:18–19
Yeast	13:33		13:20–21
Hidden treasure	13:44		
Valuable pearl	13:45–46		
Net	13:47–50		
Owner of a house	13:52		
Lost sheep	18:12–14		15:4–7
Unmerciful servant	18:23–34		
Workers in the vineyard	20:1–16		
Two sons	21:28–32		
Tenants	21:33–44	12:1–11	20:9–18
Wedding banquet	22:2–14		
Fig tree	24:32–35	13:28–29	21:29–31
Faithful and wise servant	24:45–51		12:42–48
Ten virgins	25:1–13		
Bags of gold (minas)	25:14–30		19:12–27
Sheep and goats	25:31–46		
Growing seed		4:26–29	
Watchful servants		13:35–37	12:35–40

⌇ PARABLES OF JESUS ⌇			
Parable	**Matthew**	**Mark**	**Luke**
Moneylender			7:41–43
Good Samaritan			10:30–37
Friend in need			11:5–8
Rich fool			12:16–21
Unfruitful fig tree			13:6–9
Lowest seat at the feast			14:7–17
Great banquet			14:16–24
Cost of discipleship			14:28–33
Lost coin			15:8–10
Lost (prodigal) son			15:11–32
Shrewd manager			16:1–8
Rich man and Lazarus			16:19–31
Master and his servant			17:7–10
Persistent widow			18:2–8
Pharisee and tax collector			18:10–14

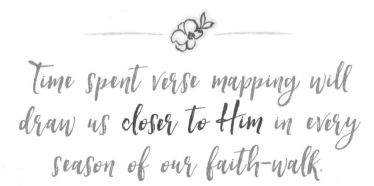

Time spent verse mapping will draw us closer to Him in every season of our faith-walk.

SESSION 5

4 *actions*   What actions develop the story in this verse? What is happening in this verse? To whom?

5 *outcome* _____

What is God saying to me today? How do I apply this to my life?

1 *verse* What verse am I mapping? What key themes or specific words are speaking to me today?

2 *design* ——————— *develop* **3**

What different  translations make up the design for this verse? Underline key phrases or words repeated.

What is the Hebrew or Greek meaning for the underlined phrases or words?

4 *actions*

What actions develop the story in this verse? What is happening in this verse? To whom?

5 *outcome*

What is God saying to me today? How do I apply this to my life?

1 *verse*   What verse am I mapping? What key themes or specific words are speaking to me today?

2 *design*  ——————— *develop* **3**

What different translations make up the design for this verse? Underline key phrases or words repeated.

What is the Hebrew or Greek meaning for the underlined phrases or words?

session
6

The Call

They asked each other, "Were not our hearts burning within us while he talked with us on the road and opened the Scriptures to us?"

LUKE 24:32

What if there were no barriers to STEP OUT on the story road in order to STEP IN to our calling with Him?

OPENING REFLECTION

In the midst of a story that wasn't going anywhere, a seven-mile stretch of road changes everything.

Two disciples—Cleopas and one other—are walking a dusty road to a town called Emmaus, talking about the incredible events that had occurred in Jerusalem over the weekend. They have no idea that the resurrected Christ Himself is going to show up and redeem everything they thought they've lost.

What if our FAITH, FOUNDATION, FEARS, and FAILURES could be used to unlock the truths in Scriptures and deepen our understanding of who Jesus is? We're about to find out.

GATHERING AND GETTING STARTED

Welcome back for session six of *Luke: Gathering the Goodness of God's Word.*

Whether you're meeting in your usual coffee shop corner, church fellowship hall, your home, or still on that favorite neighbor's front porch, this will remain a gathering study long after the sessions are over. We'll continue to invite the Holy Spirit into our day by opening the Word of God in the spaces we naturally gather.

This may be our final session to gather for video stories, but it's not the end of studying God's Word together. Before we wrap up this journey through the Gospel of Luke, come back together and discuss *one* of the following questions:

- *What verse(s) did you select to map, and why? How did it go?*

  or

- *What challenged you in discipleship this week? Did you need to have surrender-moments in order to pick up your cross and follow Jesus? Where are the areas you sense the Holy Spirit is drawing you into a closer walk with Him?*

GATHERING: VIDEO STORY

Play the video segment for session six. As you watch the final installment of our Gospel of Luke teaching, follow the verse mapping guide points starting below and refer to the completed map on pages 116–117. Take brief notes or record questions that might lead you to further research in your independent study time this week as well as in your study time in the future.

Notes

1 *verse*

What stands out in these verses:

Jesus' sharing of the Word with the disciples on the road to Emmaus is a fire-starter for their understanding. They don't want Him to leave once He's shared truth with them.

We have the same access to truth that the disciples had on the road to Emmaus. It's possible for us to walk a similar road with Jesus and have these same truths opened fully—to the extent they're revealed all the way across—from one point to the other.

The Gospel of Luke concludes with the call for disciples to GO therefore and MAKE disciples of all nations (the Great Commission)—found in Luke 24:36–49. Jesus calls us to do the same—to move past the barriers, STEP OUT on a new story road, and STEP IN to our calling with Him.

② design

"And they said to one another, 'Did not our heart burn within us while He talked with us on the road, and while He opened the Scriptures to us?'" (NKJV)

Other translations: "Back and forth they talked. 'Didn't we feel on fire as he conversed with us on the road, as he opened up the Scriptures for us?'" (MSG) "They said to one another, 'Were not our hearts burning within us while He was speaking to us on the road, while He was explaining the Scriptures to us?'" (NASB)

❸ *develop*

In the Greek, *kaió* (S. 2545) means "to ignite; burn; consume with fire; to light (a wick) and keep burning"

In the classical Greek, *laleó* (S. 2980) means more of a chatter, but the New Testament implies a more distinguished use of the word. Jesus isn't engaging in idle chitchat; He's proclaiming truths of the Scriptures.

In the Greek, *dianoigó* (S. 1272) means "to open FULLY; all the way across"

❹ *actions*

Jesus predicted His death and resurrection on multiple occasions (Luke 9:21–22; 9:43–45; 18:31–33). The disciples step out on a new story road—in faith:

Disciples believe resurrection claims are "idle tales"; Peter runs to the tomb (Luke 24:11–12)

Luke gives only reference to the road as "Emmaus" (Luke 24:13)

Disciples are downcast (Luke 24:17) but listen as Jesus opens the Scriptures to them (Luke 24:27)

Jesus gives the Great Commission—to GO and MAKE disciples (Luke 24:36–49)

5 *outcome*

It's our call—as disciples (students, learners, and ardent followers)—to GO and MAKE learners who walk in authentic discipleship with Jesus and FEAST on His Word every day.

⇒ | *Jesus gives the Great Commission— to go and make disciples.* | ⇐

4  *Can we STEP OUT in faith (on our own seven-mile road) to STEP IN to God's will?*

Jesus predicted His death and resurrection on multiple occasions (Luke 9:21–22; 9:43–45; 18:31–33). The disciples step out on a new story road—in faith:

- *While they initially thought the resurrection claims were "idle tales," Peter runs to the tomb (Luke 24:11–12)*

- *Only reference to the road as "Emmaus" (Luke 24:13)—travelers (disciples) are downcast (Luke 24:17) but listen as Jesus opens the Scriptures to them (Luke 24:27)*

- *Jesus gives the Great Commission—to go and make disciples (Luke 24:36–49) . . . also Mark 16:14–18, Matthew 28:16–20, and John 20:19–23, and in Luke's sequel, Acts 1:6–8*

5 *outcome*

It's our call – as disciples (students, learners, and ardent followers) – to GO and MAKE learners who walk in authentic discipleship with Jesus . . . and FEAST on His Word every day.

① *verse*   LUKE 24:32 (NIV)

"Were not our hearts <u>burning within us</u> while <u>He talked</u> with us on the road and <u>opened the Scriptures</u> to us?"

② *design* ——— *develop* ③

- *NKJV: "And they said to one another, 'Did not our heart <u>burn within us</u> while <u>He talked</u> with us on the road, and while <u>He opened the Scriptures</u> to us?'"*

- **BURNING**—*kaió (S. 2545):*

  "to ignite; burn; consume with fire" and "to light (a wick) and keep burning"

- **TALK**—*laleó (S. 2980):*

  "chatter" but in the New Testament it implies a more distinguished use of the word

- **OPENED**—*dianoigó (S. 1272):*

  "to open FULLY; all the way across"

▶| From the Video |◀

I'd arrived at the airport and made it through the security checkpoints two hours early—which almost never happens.

After a whirlwind weekend of signing books, of meeting readers and spending time with dear friends at a writing conference, the introvert in me was desperate for a little recharging. Quiet sounded like heaven. But with the bustle of travelers, loud speakers barking flights, and endless activity all around, an airport is the last place to go looking for peace-filled moments.

Craving any retreat, I found a deserted terminal and set myself to wait in a row of empty chairs against the wall. But I couldn't seem to latch onto a sense of peace. It had been an amazing weekend, but what kept rolling through my mind was something a friend had said before I'd left for the conference. His words were: "Walk with expectancy. We have to walk with the posture that when we expect God to move, He will." If I needed peace, then what would happen if I expected Him to provide it—especially when it seemed the least likely place to receive it?

An unfamiliar boldness rose in my heart. To date, I'd never tried to STEP OUT and harness that kind of God-movement in my life so I might STEP IN to His will over mine. I told Him: "I'm here. I'm available and I'm expectant. There's a reason You brought me to this terminal today. I believe you have a God-appointment on my schedule. So I'm just going to sit here and do my verse mapping until you bring someone to me who needs Jesus just as much as I do."

⇒| We pray for the Word
to be opened. |⇐

GATHERING: GROUP DISCUSSION

Take a few moments with your group to discuss the video you just watched and explore these concepts in Scripture.

1. Think about what it would be like to journey the seven-mile road from Jerusalem to Emmaus in the days after Jesus' crucifixion. Without social media or smart phones to spread the news in a first-century world, what would it have been like to learn that the Messiah who was supposed to deliver Israel had been executed instead? What does it feel like to encounter a hopeless situation—especially when expectations were so high in the beginning?

   _____

   _____

   _____

   _____

2. Read Luke 24:1–12. In the aftermath of Jesus' crucifixion, reports of His resurrection reach the disciples with a combination of doubt and hope. But Peter—in desperate need of restoration—runs to the tomb without delay. How does Peter's experience with hope differ from the disciples' on the road to Emmaus? Does finally seeing Christ's resurrected body help redeem what he'd lost by denying Him?

   _____

   _____

   _____

   _____

3. Even though Jesus predicted His death and resurrection on multiple occasions (Luke 9:21–22; 9:43–45; 18:31–33), Luke 24 opens in the aftermath of what appears to be THE END of what the disciples had given up everything for. They're reeling from loss, but Jesus steps in with the victory when they thought there was none to be found. How did Jesus restore the disciples' hope in a completely hopeless situation? How could He do the same for us?

_____

_____

_____

_____

_____

4. Select a volunteer (or more than one) to read the accounts of the Great Commission in Mark 16:14–18, Matthew 28:16–20, John 20:19–23, and Acts 1:6–8 aloud to the group. How are we empowered to go and make disciples? Is there anything that can hold us back from sharing the gospel with travelers we might meet?

_____

_____

_____

_____

Define "hope." What does it mean to you?

_____

_____

_____

GATHERING: GROUP ACTIVITY

For this activity, each participant will need a Bible, pens/markers, and a smart device (such as a phone or tablet).

● Using a Bible or Bible app on a smart device, look up two additional translations of Luke 24:32, and record them on the completed map on pages 116–117.

● To continue your verse mapping journey, pray as a group and select one verse you'll map in self-study time this week. And talk about gathering again after this study is over. A coffee shop corner, a Bible, a notebook and pens, and friends with open hearts—it's all you need to keep going.

GATHERING: CLOSING PRAYER

Every verse mapping experience begins and ends with prayer.

We end session six the same way we began—praying that Jesus would be our companion; our steadfast, servant leader; and our fire-starter to GO and MAKE disciples. Whether it's a six-week journey or a trek down a seven-mile road, we pray for more of Jesus.

We pray for the Word to be opened, and nothing to stamp out the flame in our heart.

See for yourself how intimately your heavenly Father is involved in each chapter of your story!

session 6

INDIVIDUAL STUDY

The Call

They asked each other, "Were not our hearts burning within us while
he talked with us on the road and opened the Scriptures to us?"

LUKE 24:32

What if there were no barriers to STEP OUT on the story road in order to STEP IN to our calling with Him?

GATHER: INDIVIDUAL STUDY INVITATION

This is the week where you experience the seven-mile walk to Emmaus, in Luke 24.

Everything you believe in hinges on this road because it's where the Scriptures are opened. Fully. In your mind and hands and heart, as you turn pages and map truths. You will be front and center for the resurrection (24:1–12)—the reason we have hope! You'll experience the depth of redemption as Peter runs to an empty tomb (24:12), and revival as the disciples' eyes are opened (24:28–35). What seemed like the ending was a new beginning all along. And what the disciples learned is everything we have at our fingertips. It's here. In the same words you're taking in, and the same truths you're living out.

Dig your heels into this earth, because the harvest is calling.

Read

LUKE 24

Pray. We are deep in the GATHERING. Jesus has summoned us and we're shouldering our cross day by day. Whether it's five minutes today or an hour tomorrow, invite the Holy Spirit and gather with Him. Seek God's face in the verse(s) you will map this week.

Read Luke 24. Let this week shake you. Let it stir a deep longing in your heart. Now that you know how, keep walking with Him. Don't let the mapping journey end—let it flourish within you in the same way His disciples are called to begin (24:46–53).

When you've finished mapping your verses this week, turn to to the "Story Road through Luke" section, located behind your blank maps. There you'll find space to record the journey you've been on—to document the outcomes and lay out the entire map you've encountered in the Gospel of Luke. Gather your verses and your outcomes, and see for yourself how intimately your heavenly Father is involved in each chapter of your story!

Study Support Examples

Information you might find in your research . . .

24:1–53 *Resurrection and Ascension of Jesus.* Luke provides the basis of the early Christian confession: "You killed the author of life, but God raised him from the dead. We are witnesses of this" (Acts 3:15). Luke begins with the discovery of the empty tomb (vv. 1–12); discusses the meaning of Jesus' death and resurrection (vv. 13–35); links his life, death, and resurrection to the disciples' continued mission as his witnesses (vv. 36–49); and ends with Jesus' ascension (vv. 50–53), reserving a more detailed description for the beginning of his second volume (Acts 1:1–11).

Excerpted from *NIV Theology Study Bible.* Copyright © 2015, 2018, Zondervan.

4 *actions*   What actions develop the story in this verse? What is happening in this verse? To whom?

5 *outcome*

What is God saying to me today? How do I apply this to my life?

1 *verse* What verse am I mapping? What key themes or specific words are speaking to me today?

2 *design* ——————— *develop* 3

What different translations make up the design for this verse? Underline key phrases or words repeated.

What is the Hebrew or Greek meaning for the underlined phrases or words?

4 *actions*

What actions develop the story in this verse? What is happening in this verse? To whom?

5 *outcome*

What is God saying to me today? How do I apply this to my life?

1 *verse*   What verse am I mapping? What key themes or specific words are speaking to me today?

2 *design* ——————— *develop* **3**

What different translations make up the design for this verse? Underline key phrases or words repeated.

What is the Hebrew or Greek meaning for the underlined phrases or words?

Verse mapping reveals our personal story roads with the Holy Spirit, just as it reveals deep truths in Scripture.

STORY ROAD THROUGH
Luke

Verse mapping reveals our personal story roads with the Holy Spirit, just as it reveals deep truths in Scripture. It's going to happen in the moments of spontaneity—dependent on the Holy Spirit's direction—and in the journeys that result from your curiosity in study.

STORY ROAD INSTRUCTIONS

<u>Write each verse we mapped</u> through our study in the Gospel of Luke. (Starting with Luke 1:45, include every verse Kristy mapped in her teaching, the verses your group mapped together, and those verses you mapped in your self-study time.)

<u>Rewrite the Outcome statement</u> from each map through our study in the Gospel of Luke. (Starting with session one's *"Who Jesus became and what He fulfilled were, in part, triggered by the blessing—the favor of God on the world—and in 'she who BELIEVED,'"* include each outcome from Kristy's teachings, the outcome from each of your group maps, and each outcome from your self-study maps.)

<u>Read over your entire journey</u>—the outcomes that you'll refer back to over time. What message has the Holy Spirit revealed to you? Where has God breathed truth into your life, and how will you use that truth to impact this season? Remember, God meets you every time you engage Him on your story road, and He longs to walk every step of the journey alongside you!

<u>Return to these truths.</u> Come back to the Word with this approach. It's personal, crafted from His heart to yours. And it's not meant to stay in a study guide book that gets tucked away on a shelf. Imagine you're on that seven-mile road and Jesus opens the Word. We wouldn't want Him to leave!

This may be our last gathering, but that's not where the discipleship ends.

video maps

What are the (6) Scripture verses we mapped in the video stories? Write them here:

VERSE(S)

---

group maps

What are the Scripture verses I mapped together with my group? Write them here:

VERSE(S)

What are the (6) Outcomes from mapping in the video stories?
Write them here:

OUTCOME STATEMENTS

_____

_____

_____

_____

_____

_____

What are the (6) Outcomes from mapping with my group?
Write them here:

OUTCOME STATEMENTS

_____

_____

_____

_____

_____

_____

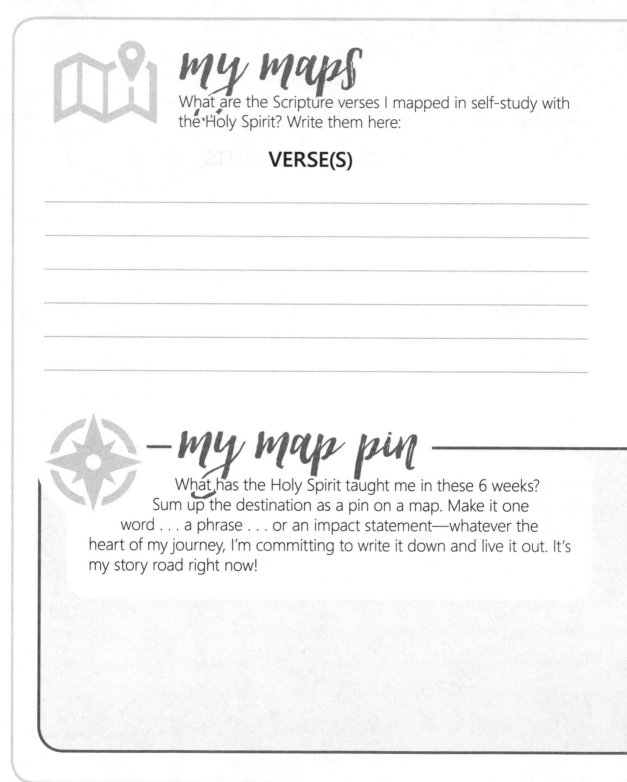

my maps

What are the Scripture verses I mapped in self-study with the Holy Spirit? Write them here:

VERSE(S)

_____

_____

_____

_____

_____

_____

— my map pin —

What has the Holy Spirit taught me in these 6 weeks? Sum up the destination as a pin on a map. Make it one word . . . a phrase . . . or an impact statement—whatever the heart of my journey, I'm committing to write it down and live it out. It's my story road right now!

What are the (6) Outcomes from mapping in self-study with the Holy Spirit? Write them here:

OUTCOME STATEMENTS

VERSE MAPPING STUDY PLANS
Gospel of Luke

Ready to gather again? Grab your verse mapping journal and get your discipleship on in a new mapping journey! Gathering the Goodness study plans for the Gospel of Luke are here:

on FAITH:

- Luke 5:12–14
- Luke 5:17–26
- Luke 5:27–28
- Luke 7:36–39
- Luke 9:18–20
- Luke 18:35–43

on PARABLES:

- Luke 8:4–8
- Luke 8:16
- Luke 10:25–37
- Luke 13:18–19
- Luke 15:1–7
- Luke 15:11–31

on HEALING:

- Luke 4:31–37
- Luke 5:12–16
- Luke 5:40–41
- Luke 8:46–48
- Luke 13:10–17
- Luke 18:35–43

verse mapping
Reference and Resource Guide

RESOURCES TO HELP YOU STUDY THE BIBLE LIKE NEVER BEFORE

BOOKS

- *The NKJV Study Bible, 2nd Edition* (Thomas Nelson), by Earl D. Radmacher (editor), Ronald B. Allen (editor), H. Wayne House (editor)

- *NIV Chronological Study Bible* (Thomas Nelson)

- *NIV Biblical Theology Study Bible* (Zondervan), D. A. Carson (general editor)

- *The NIV Exhaustive Bible Concordance, Third Edition: A Better Strong's Bible Concordance* (Zondervan), by John R. Kohlenberger III

- *Mounce's Complete Expository Dictionary of Old and New Testament Words* (Zondervan), by William D. Mounce (general editor)

- Concordance, if other biblical translations are preferred (NASB, KJV, MSG, etc.)

- Other Bible studies—these books/study guides that are gathering dust on the shelves could be a gold mine of information when researching. Get them out and use them!

WEBSITES

- BibleGateway.com—free biblical translations, Hebrew/Greek lexicon, commentaries, concordance(s), biblical dictionaries

- BibleHub.com—great word search site, Hebrew/Greek lexicon

- Logos.com—free and paid in-depth biblical resource site

- YouTube.com—videos of sites/locations being researched

*ALWAYS utilize references/websites that come from reputable sources (i.e., NOT an online crowd-sourcing encyclopedia). It is okay to use whatever websites pop up in a Google search—as long as they contain evidence you can confirm. Approved websites could be, for example: university/seminary websites, or sites that contain articles from recognized research/news sources (History.com, Smithsonian, National Geographic, museums or historical institutions, etc.).

HISTORY BOOKS AND MAPS

Your local library can be an invaluable resource for:

- Greco-Roman art, archaeology, and history books

- Maps and in-depth historical context on life and culture in a first-century Roman world

- Anything that includes timelines, maps, etc. of the ancient world will add to your research

The point of all of this is to **think like a researcher.** *Be curious. Ask questions. Dig for answers. Don't just accept an answer—use it as a springboard to research on your own.*

SMALL GROUP OR CHURCH MEMBERS/LEADERS

- Someone who is seminary trained by education/vocation

- Someone who has walked with Jesus for many years—even in ministry—and may have valuable insight into the topic you're researching

- A member who has studied Hebrew/Greek (wowza, if you do!)—or Jewish culture

- Someone who learned what you're discussing in another Bible study

Bottom line—use the resources/sphere of influence within your reach!
ASK QUESTIONS. Own your faith in Jesus; the learning is up to you. :-)

Community Connections

Need more help? Go to versemapping.com or search the following social media hashtags to find other mappers who've shared their mapping journeys online. You'll find support and collaboration in a space that's always available.

#VerseMapping

#VerseMapclub

#GoandMakeChallenge (community maps from *Luke: Gathering the Goodness of God's Word*)

#FeastandFullChallenge (community maps from *Acts: Feasting on the Abundance of God's Word*)

Acknowledgments

From the beginning of this verse mapping journey, we said we wanted to write about Jesus. That if there were only six stories we could tell a traveler who wanted *more*—let it be these.

For the friends who believed in this project (the blessed are they who believed!): John Raymond, Rachelle Gardner, Daisy Hutton . . .

For the servant leaders who step back in line, supporting as mentors and faithful friends: Katherine and Sarah, Beth, Jeane, Colleen, Bex, Allen, Sharon, Maggie, Eileen, Marlene, Kerry, Joyce, Kelli, Gary and Lanette . . .

For the incredible production team who traveled every inch of the seven-mile road in this study: Mark Weising, Sara Riemersma, Brookwater Films, 52 Watt Studios, Robin Crosslin, and Greg Clouse . . .

For the precious-to-me who considered the cost of discipleship, and gave, gave, gave of themselves to make His Name great: Rick and Linda, Jenny, Jeremy, Brady, Carson, and Colt . . .

And for the One who gave it all in hopes we'd one day want to gather with Him . . .

. . . THANK YOU is never enough. (But it's a start.) I love you.